EXPERIMENT WITH WEATHER

Written by **Miranda Bower**

Science Consultant Bob Aran
Regional Commercial Manager, London Weather Centre,
The Met. Office
Education Consultant Ruth Bessant

TWO-CAN

This edition first published in Great Britain in 1992 by
Two-Can Publishing Ltd
346 Old Street
London EC1V 9NQ
in association with Scholastic Publications Ltd

Printed and bound in Hong Kong

2 4 6 8 10 9 7 5 3 1

A catalogue record for this book is available from the British library

(Pbk) ISBN: 1-85434-124-3
(Hbk) ISBN: 1-85434-159-6

Photograph credits:
Cover: Oxford Scientific Films/Warren Faidley
Bruce Coleman (Flip de Nooyer) 4 (left), (Norbert Rosing) 5 (top), 10, 12, (John Shaw) 20 (bottom), 22 (bottom), (David Davies) 25 (top); Steve Davey 23 (top); Frank Lane Picture Agency (R. Bird) 18 (bottom); NHPA (Martin Wendler) 15 (top); Oxford Scientific Films (Warren Faidley) cover, 18 (top), (Stan Osolinski) 13, 20 (top), (Ronald Toms) 14 (top), (Paul Franklin) 25 (top); Planet Earth Pictures (Mark Mattock) 14 (bottom); Science Photo Library (Dr Fred Espenak) 6 (left), (John Mead) 11/12 (background), (Peter Menzel) 27 (bottom right); Science Photo Library /European Space Agency 6 (left), Zefa 21 (top), 5 (left), (Art Wolfe) 9, (Wienke) 10, (Photri) 16, (R. Lincks) 28 (bottom right), (Damm) 29 (bottom left), (Ernst A. Weber) 29 (top left).

All other photographs by Paul Bricknell

Illustrations by Nancy Anderson. Design by Eve White. Art directed by Fionna Robson. Edited by Monica Byles and Amanda Pratt.

Thanks to the staff and pupils of St George's School Hanover Square, London W1. Thanks also to Siobhán Power.

CONTENTS

Sky cycle	4
Weather watch	6
Round and round	8
Heavens above	10
Rain drain	12
Flood gates	14
Howling winds	16
Thunder and lightning	18
Snow and ice	20
Heat and drought	22
Weather damage	24
Simple seasons	26
The weather and you	28
Glossary	30
Index	32

All words marked in **bold** can be found in the glossary

SKY CYCLE

What's the weather like? Cold and wet or warm and sunny? We need to know because weather affects us in many ways – what we wear, what we eat, even how we travel.

▶ The world is divided into different areas of weather zones. The zones differ depending on how close they are to the Equator, how far they are from the coast, and how high the land is.

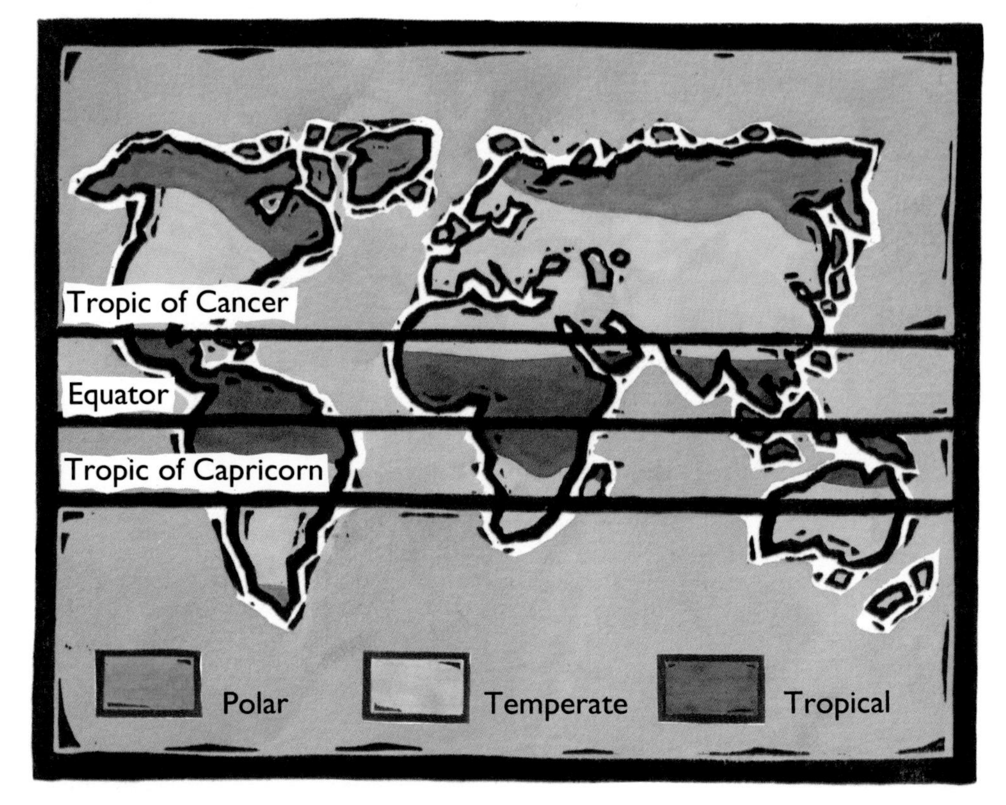

▲ Without the heat of the Sun, our world would be cold, lifeless and frozen. How much sunshine we receive depends on where we live on the planet.

◀ **Meteorology** is the science of weather. The word comes from the Greek **meteoron** which means 'strange events in the sky'. One of the stangest sorts of weather are auroras, flashing lights in the night sky that occur close to the Earth's north and south poles.

▼ The warmth of the Sun lifts moisture from oceans, lakes and rivers. This water in the atmosphere makes the rain, fog and snow. How do you protect yourself in wet weather?

▲ When layers of air are heated by the Sun's rays, they become lighter and rise. Cooler, heavier air rushes in to take their place, and so winds are formed. Some parts of the world have very strong winds. The most violent are known as **hurricanes**. These usually begin over warm parts of the world's oceans.

WEATHER WATCH

Did you hear the **weather forecast** today? How can a forecaster know what the weather is going to be like? Forecasts are made by studying **data** collected at weather stations around the world. The information comes from meteorologists, and from instruments carried in balloons, planes or satellites.

▲ Computers inside weather stations help to work out what all the data means. The information is plotted on a map called a synoptic chart. This is a computer picture of a hurricane, built up from signals beamed to Earth from a weather satellite. Satellites collect information which cannot be seen from the ground, such as cloud coverage over a wide area.

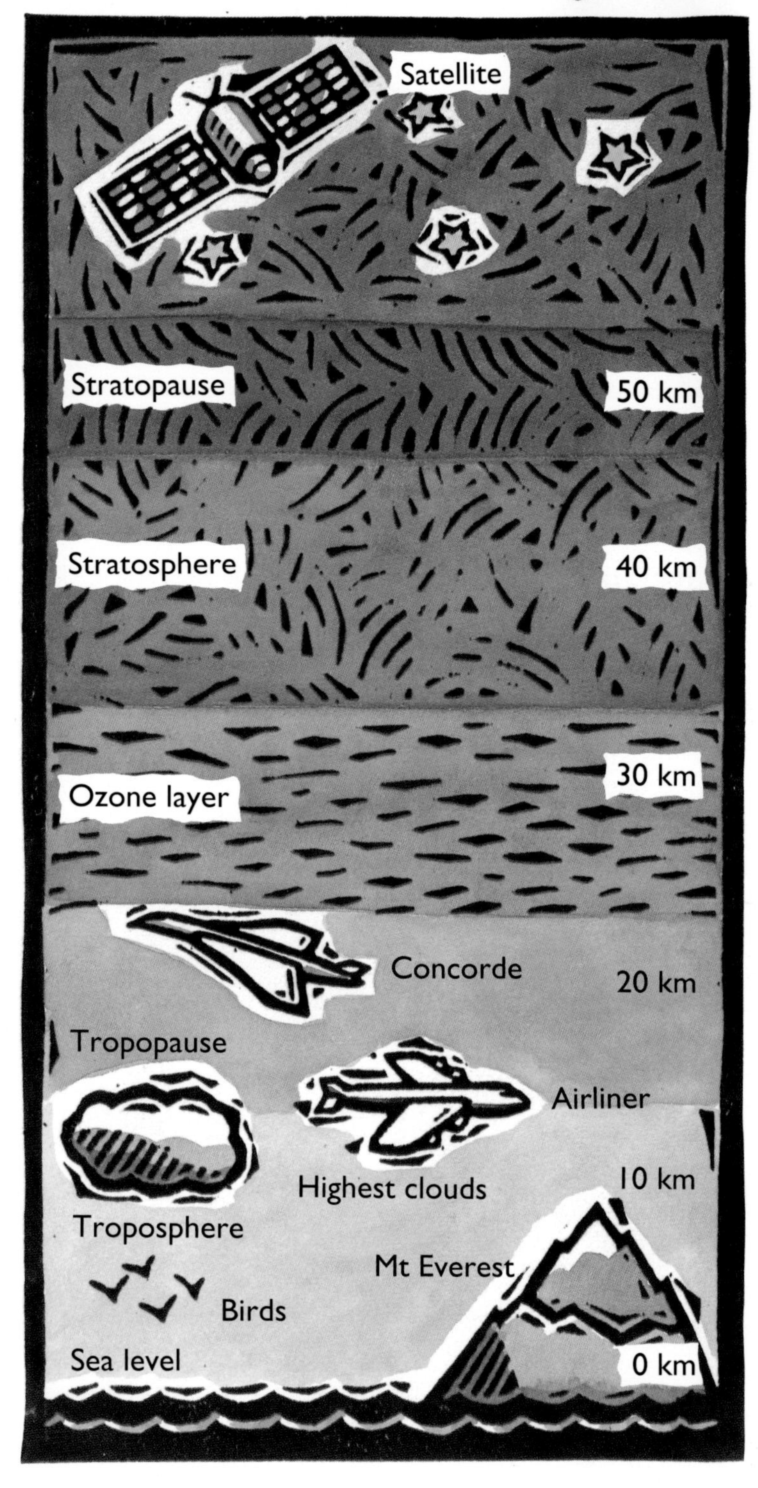

▲ The Earth is surrounded by a thin layer of gases which protect us from feeling extremes of heat and cold. The layer nearest to the Earth is the troposphere, where weather develops.

▶ Nature sometimes has its own ways of forecasting the weather. Pine cones open when it is warm (to let their seeds fall out), but on cold days they stay closed.

▼ Satellite photographs show the Earth from outside the **atmosphere**. All satellites **orbit** the Earth, going round and round the planet in a giant loop. Some orbit low down, others circle the Earth much higher up.

▲ Weather balloons float high into the atmosphere. They carry radio probes and transmit details of the **temperature** and dampness of the air.

▼ If you ever go to the seaside, bring back some seaweed. Fix a strand outside, near a door or window. When rain is due, the seaweed will grow damp and limp. In sunny weather it will turn crispy and dry.

ROUND AND ROUND

◀ Hang out wet clothes on a warm, breezy day and before long they are dry. The water has evaporated. This means it has changed into invisible water **vapour** – tiny drops of water in the air which you cannot see. There is always some water vapour in the air, even in deserts.

▶ On farms in hot regions of Australia, the precious water is stored in open tanks, covered by floating plastic balls. Rain collects in the tanks, but sunshine reflects off the white balls. Less water evaporates and so less water is lost.

▼ Pour equal amounts of water into two identical containers. Cover the surface of the water in one container with polystyrene beads. Leave both containers in a sunny spot which is protected from the wind. After several days measure the water from each container. Which lost more water? Do you know why this could be?

▲ In the cold of night, some water vapour in the air may condense and settle as drops of **dew**. As the Sun comes up, it gets warmer and the dew begins to **evaporate**.

HEAVEN IS ABOVE

Did you know that cloud watching can tell you what weather lies ahead? Puffy white cumulus clouds are common in summer. In a blue sky, they rarely bring rain. If they cover most of the sky, rain is more likely to fall.

▲ Fog is an ordinary cloud, lying close to ground level. It often forms on still, cool mornings.

▼ Try making a cloud in a bottle. Ask an adult to fill a jar with hot water, leave it for a moment, then pour most away. Put ice on some thin material stretched over the top of the jar. A cloud will form as the warm and cold air meet.

▲ Cumulo-nimbus clouds bring thunderstorms with heavy showers of rain.

▲ Even in fine weather, wispy cirrus clouds can show rain is coming.

▲ Thick, flat stratus clouds often bring drizzle and are usually associated with bad weather.

RAIN DRAIN

Rain comes to us as part of the **water cycle**. The Sun's heat draws up water vapour from seas, rivers and lakes. As it rises and cools, the vapour forms a cloud, which rises higher and higher, meeting cold air. Raindrops form and fall back to the ground, draining into rivers and the sea, where the cycle begins all over again.

The Water Cycle

▼ Fill a jar with water and rest it on a sunny window sill. Move white paper next to the jar, until you see bright colours reflected on it. The water in the jar splits the sunlight into the seven colours of the **rainbow**.

▲ The tiny water droplets in a cloud collide, and eventually join to form larger drops of rainwater. A raindrop may contain about one million cloud droplets before it is heavy enough to fall.

▼ If there is a shower while the Sun is still shining, the individual raindrops can split the **light** of the Sun into an arc of coloured bands called a rainbow. The bands always come in the same order of red, orange, yellow, green, blue, indigo and violet.

FLOOD GATES

Most floods are caused by heavy rain. Rivers swell and burst their banks, pouring water on to the surrounding land.

▶ Sometimes, a valley is flooded on purpose by building a **dam** across one end. A **reservoir** of water forms behind the dam. In a **hydro-electric** dam, water rushes through holes in the dam to make electricity.

◀ A sudden flood may cut off communities, destroy homes, kill animals and people, and ruin crops. Some countries suffer flooding disasters every few years.

▶ Make a gauge to measure how much it rains. Fit a funnel into the neck of a jar and put it outside to collect the water. You could bury the jar in the ground to keep it upright. Each week, pour the rainwater into a measuring jug and compare how much rain has fallen.

▶ Flooding isn't always bad news, so long as farmers have enough warning and time to prepare for the flood. In many parts of the world, such as on this farm in Brazil, rivers break their banks during each rainy season. The waters carry particles of rock, worn away from the river bed. When the water finally goes down, valleys are covered in a rich mud, excellent for growing crops.

HOWLING WINDS

Is the wind blowing now? Sometimes it just gently flutters leaves, at other times it blows up a gale.

▼ A tornado forms when warm air rises rapidly and is replaced by more warm air. A tunnel of air is sucked up and then starts to spin round.

Air can be cold, warm, damp or dry, depending on the land and sea below it. Warm air rises, and cold, heavy air rushes in to take its place, making a wind. The edges of large masses of air are called **fronts**. Clouds and rain often form where cold and warm fronts meet.

In 1805, Admiral Sir Francis Beaufort invented a scale to measure wind speed at sea. This version was for use on land.

To make a weather vane, tape paper arrow shapes to the ends of a straw. Ask an adult to pin it to a stick or pencil. Push the stick through the bottom of a large yoghurt pot. Fix the pot with modelling clay in a level, windy place. Use a compass to mark north, south, east and west.

THE BEAUFORT SCALE

1. Calm: smoke drifts around, wind does not move weather vanes.
2. Wind is felt on the face. Leaves rustle, vanes move.
3. Leaves and twigs move. Flags flap.
4. Wind lifts dust and loose paper, and moves small branches.
5. Small leafy trees sway. Wavelets form on water.
6. Large branches move. Telegraph wires hum. Umbrellas blow about.
7. Trees sway. Walking into the wind is difficult.
8. Gale: twigs snap off trees.
9. Strong gale: roof tiles blow off.
10. Storm: trees are uprooted, buildings are damaged.
11. Violent storm with widespread damage.
12. Hurricane at sea.

THUNDER AND LIGHTNING

Weather forecasters chart the progress of heavy rain, strong winds and thunder so that they can send out **storm warnings**. Then people living in the danger zones can take steps to protect their homes or crops.

▼ This charred tree was scorched by lightning. Storms damage property and livestock every year.

▲ Lightning is caused by a giant build-up of **static electricity** inside a thunder cloud. Eventually, the electricity breaks out as a streak of lightning. It takes the fastest route to earth, and often strikes tall buildings and trees.

▶ Many buildings are fitted with a metal strip called a **lightning conductor**. This leads lightning safely to the ground.

▼ Static electricity doesn't just cause lightning. You can see it in action in other ways too. Rub a balloon on your clothes and then press it against a smooth wall. Static electricity will make it cling to the wall.

SNOW AND ICE

In very cold clouds, water vapour turns into tiny crystals of ice. As the crystals bump into one another, they join up and become snowflakes.

▲ **Hailstones** form in cumulo-nimbus clouds. Particles of ice move about in the cloud, gathering layers of ice. When hail is heavy, it falls. The biggest stone recorded was the size of a melon.

▲ When **condensation** or vapour freezes, it forms **frost**. **Rime** is formed when water drops in fog freeze on cold objects.

◀ Next time it snows, look at some snowflakes through a magnifying glass. Every crystal has six sides but each one is different. Some are rod-shaped, but others are much more intricate.

▲ These sheep have thick coats to protect them from the cold. In the spring, as the weather gets warmer, the sheep no longer need these fleecy coats. They are shorn by the farmer, to provide us with wool.

Do not use a glass bottle. It might explode.

▶ Fill a plastic bottle to the brim with water. (Make sure it is plastic and not glass.) Screw the lid on tight and put the bottle in the freezer. After a while, the sides will bulge and crack – when water freezes it **expands**. That is why water pipes are **lagged** in winter to keep them warm and stop them bursting.

HEAT AND DROUGHT

Droughts happen when there is much less rain than usual. Water supplies run low, and if the drought is severe, crops, animals and even people may die. Another problem is that fertile soil may turn to dust and blow away.

▶ The world's desert regions are dry all year round. However, crops can be grown in an **oasis**, or on land that has been artificially **irrigated**.

◀ In the desert, a year's rainfall may come in a single downpour. Some desert plants grow and flower very quickly.

▶ To make a sundial, cut out a large circle of card. Then draw a right-angled triangle with a flap and cut it out. Fold back the flap and glue it to the circle. Out of doors, use a compass to line up the sundial on a north-south line. Each hour, mark where the shadow falls on the circle of card.

◀ Aeroplanes often fly above cloud level. The sky is always clear there, even if it is raining below.

▶ A **thermometer** measures temperature on either the **Celsius** or **Fahrenheit** scale. Liquid at the bottom expands with warmth and moves up the tube. The level it reaches on the scale shows the temperature.

WEATHER DAMAGE

The Earth is surrounded by layers of different gases. These form the **atmosphere.** They include a gas called carbon dioxide, which helps to keep our planet at the correct temperature.

◀ Our climate changes naturally but very slowly. However, scientists now think that the way we live is affecting the delicate balance of gases in the atmosphere, causing weather patterns to change more quickly than normal.

▼ Trees need carbon dioxide to make food. If we destroy rainforests there are fewer trees using up less carbon dioxide which can cause weather changes.

◀ The Earth's climate is affected by **pollution**, especially air pollution. Car exhausts, factories and power stations pump waste gases out into the air. Many of these gases mix with water vapour in clouds. They make the rain much more acid, so that sometimes the rainwater actually damages the environment. Acid rain poisons rivers and lakes. It kills trees and even eats away at the stonework on buildings.

▶ How acid is your local rainfall? To find out ask an adult to boil half a red cabbage in water. Leave it to soak for several hours, then strain the liquid into a dish. Soak strips of white blotting paper in the juice and let them dry. These can be used to test for acids. Dip seperate strips into the juice of a lemon, tap water and rainwater. The stronger the acid in the liquid, the pinker your testing strip will be.

SIMPLE SEASONS

Have you ever wondered why parts of the world have different patterns of cold and warm weather which vary throughout the year?

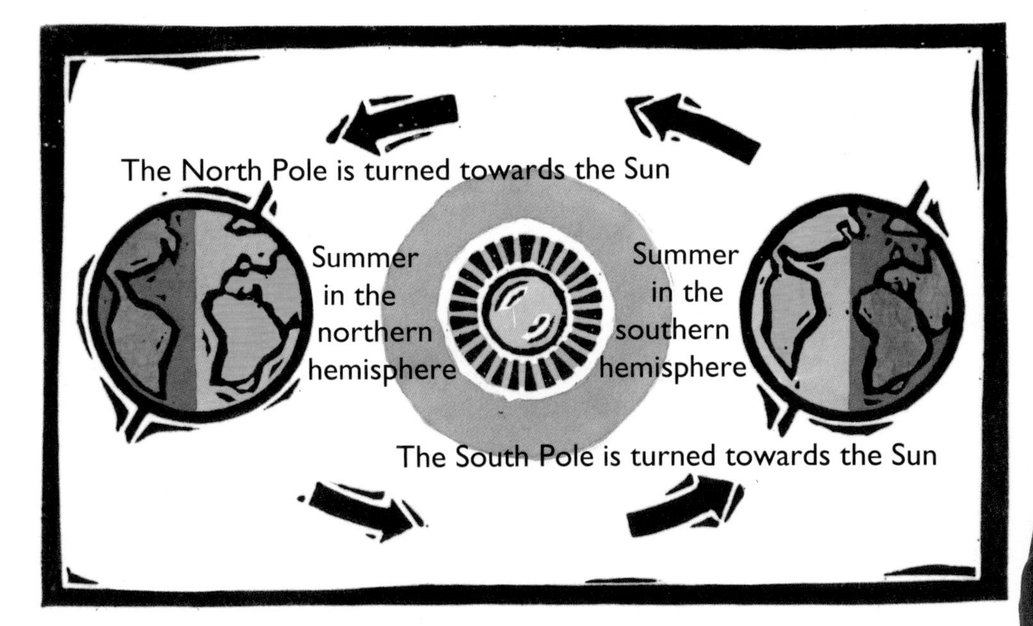

▲ The Earth orbits the Sun in one year, spinning slowly as it goes. The Earth's **seasons** are caused as the different parts of the Earth's surface are tilted towards the Sun. As regions lean from its warmth, they experience winter.

Temperate regions of the world have four seasons: spring, summer, autumn and winter. Tropical areas, near the Equator, are hot all year round, but they may still have two seasons – a dry one and a rainy one.

▼ Some animals travel to warm regions before winter comes. These Monarch butterflies **migrate** 3,000 km each year from North to South America.

◀ People also change habits with the seasons. In winter we wear layers of clothing to trap heat. In summer, we put on loose clothing, skin lotions and sunglasses to protect us from the Sun.

THE WEATHER AND YOU

The weather affects us in all kinds of different ways – often more than we realize. Sunny, warm weather makes many people feel much happier than cold, wet weather. Changing seasons can affect our moods and feelings too.

▼ On summer days, many people suffer from hay fever caused by pollen which is in flowering plants.

▲ We play different sports in different seasons. Football is usually a winter sport, but it's not such fun swimming out of doors in winter weather!

▲ Many people enjoy winter sports, such as skiing. On a dry ski slope you can ski in summer.

◀ Climate affects how people live. Houses in hot countries such as Greece are often painted white, because the white colour reflects the heat. Houses may have small windows too, to keep out the sun. In cool countries, on the other hand, windows are often **double-glazed** to keep the heat in.

▲ Surveys show that windy, stormy weather often makes people grumpy. Some illnesses seem to get worse in bad weather. Chest complaints are more painful on a cold and foggy day.

GLOSSARY

Atmosphere is the thin layer of gases around the Earth.

Celsius is a measure of temperature .

Climate is the weather pattern of a region.

Condensation is when water vapour turns back to water as it cools.

Dam is a barrier that holds back water.

Data means items of information.

Dew is the drops of water that settle when vapour condenses during a cool night.

Double-glazed windows have two panes of glass that help keep warmth inside a house.

Drought is a long period when little or no rain falls on an area.

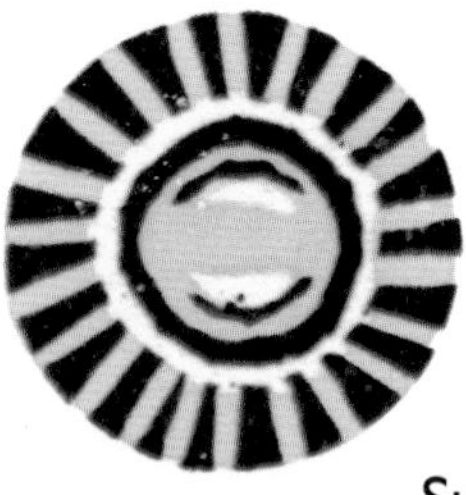

Sun

Rain cloud

Evaporate is when water changes from a liquid to invisible water vapour.

Fahrenheit is a measure of temperature.

Front is the boundary between warm air and cold air masses.

Frost is frozen dew or water vapour, which forms on flat surfaces and on the ground.

Hailstones are balls of ice that form in cold clouds and fall when they are heavy.

Hemisphere is half of the Earth. The northern hemisphere runs from the Equator to the North Pole. The southern hemisphere runs from the Equator to the South Pole.

Hurricanes are the strongest level of stormy winds.

Hydro-electric power is made when falling water turns large machines called turbines to produce electricity.

Irrigation is when water is channelled to feed crops in dry soil.

Lagged pipes are wrapped in material that restricts the amount of heat that goes out or comes in. House pipes are lagged to stop water in them from freezing and splitting the pipes.

Lightning conductor is a strip of metal, usually copper, that is fitted to the length of a tall building.

Meteorology is the study of weather.

Migration is when animals travel from their summer feeding grounds to a warmer climate before winter comes.

Oasis is an area of vegetation around water in a desert.

Orbit is to circle around something. The planet Earth orbits the Sun.

Pollution is the contamination of soil, water and air by substances that have been made by humans.

Rainbow is seen when sunlight shines through raindrops and is split into bands of the seven colours that make up light.

Reservoir is an artificial lake.

Lightning conductor

Rime is the ice crystals that freeze on to cold objects on a cold, foggy morning.

Seasons are divisions of the year with their own patterns of weather.

Static electricity is a form of electricity caused by rubbing certain materials together.

Storm warning is given by forecasters before a storm.

Temperature is a measure of how hot or cold something is. It is usually measured in degrees Fahrenheit (°F) or degrees Celsius (°C).

Thermometer is an instrument used to measure temperature.

Vapour is an invisible gas in the air. Water becomes vapour when it evaporates.

Water cycle is the process by which water from seas, rivers, lakes and swamps evaporates, forms clouds, falls as rain, snow or hail and returns to the rivers once again.

Weather forecast is a prediction of how the weather is likely to be in the near future.

INDEX

acid rain 25
atmosphere 7, 24
aurora 5

Beaufort Scale 17

climate 24, 25, 29
cloud 10, 11, 12, 17, 20, 23
condensation 20

dam 14
dew 9
drought 22

Earth 6, 7, 24, 25, 26
evaporate 9

flood 14, 15
fog 10
forecasting 6, 7, 18
fronts 17
frost 20

hail 20
hurricane 5, 6, 17
hydro-electric power 14

meteorology 4, 5
migration 27

pollution 25

rain 9-14, 17, 22, 25
rainbow 12, 13
rime 20

seasons 24 - 28
snow 20
storm 17, 18, 19
Sun 4, 5, 24, 26, 27

temperature 7, 23
thunder and lightning 18, 19
tornado 16, 17

vapour 9, 12, 20

water cycle 12, 13
wind 9, 16, 17